Where Heaven Meets Earth

(Intimacy and Impact through Prayer)

Bible Study and Prayer Guide
By Don and Vicki Twiford

Restoring God's House of Prayer Expanded
© Copyright 2014 Twiford Ministries
All right reserved

No part of this book may be reproduced in any form except by express permission of:

Twiford Ministries
P.O. Box 2417
Burleson, TX 76097-2417

Library of Congress Control Number: 2014921822
CreateSpace Independent Publishing Platform, North Charleston, SC

This expanded edition: (softcover)
ISBN-13: 978-1503233430
ISBN-10: 150323343X

Formatting by AnnMarie Stone

Note: Some Scripture quotations have been bolded, italicized or underlined for emphasis.

Contents

Where Heaven Meets Earth

The title **Where Heaven Meets Earth** was inspired by the scripture, "'Heaven is my throne and earth is my footstool' (Isa 66:1/Acts 7:49). Imagine finding the place where God's feet touch the Earth. It's not so much about finding a physical location as it is about meeting with God in the dwelling place of your Spirit, growing in intimacy with Him, and then impacting your world with the love, faith, and power that you experience in His presence.

Finding that place has been a journey of encountering God in unexpected ways, as well as a journey through scripture to help us understand the depths of those experiences. We have also gained a great deal of understanding from others who have embarked upon this same journey.

Although throughout our walk with the Lord, we have had a deep desire to grow in our relationship with the Lord, our journey of encountering His presence was greatly enhanced while attending a pastor's conference in 1996.

During the opening session, a nationally known evangelist was teaching about the golden altar of incense which was in the Old Testament Tabernacle. He used New Testament scriptures to explain how the golden altar symbolized our worship. He explained in great detail how worship was given to man by God to usher His people into His presence (covered in more detail in chapter 4).

In this minister's teaching, and throughout the conference, we repeatedly heard this phrase: 'Praise until you worship, and worship until the glory comes.' It created a desire within both of us to worship God in a deeper way, and to personally experience His glory here on this earth. And that is exactly what happened during the course of the conference.

From that time on, the desire to walk in the presence of God and experience His glory in greater measure continued to grow. Several years later, we had the privilege of hearing another great man of God tell about how 'praying through the tabernacle' revolutionized his prayer time and greatly deepened His understanding of God.

At the time, he was the pastor of the world's largest church located in Seoul, Korea. His name is Pastor David Yonggi Cho. While there are many types and models of prayer, Dr. Cho calls this particular type of prayer his 'fellowship prayer.' His teaching is based upon the pattern of the Tabernacle which is directly connected to Isaiah 56:4-7 and Mark 11:17:

*'My House will be called a house of prayer
for all nations.'*

To understand how these scriptures apply to your personal prayer life, consider the fact that the house in which you live is known as your house because you dwell there. If you were to move, it would no longer be called your house. Couple this fact with the truth that God's people are now God's dwelling place, His house through His Spirit living in them, and the conclusion must be drawn that we are to be known as a people who pray. You are to be the place Where Heaven Meets Earth in intimacy through prayer and then impact your world!

When we studied the principles taught by Dr. Cho in Scripture and began to apply these principles to our personal prayer times (sometimes once a week, and some weeks every day), we not only experienced a deepened relationship with the Lord, but also a greater revelation of our purpose and the power available to us in prayer.

We soon wrote a manual and began teaching these principles to others in churches where we ministered. It was wonderful to find that when we applied them to a corporate setting, people began longing to spend more time in prayer rather than seeing prayer as a task to check off of their to-do list.

At one church in Columbus, NE we lead the congregation in a time of prayer following the seminar. After we prayed, the youth pastor said, "Do we have to have church as usual tomorrow? Couldn't we just pray?" The pastor's wife went home and applied the same principles to her personal prayer time. She testified the next day by saying, "After praying, I thought I was in the presence of the Lord for just a few minutes. But when I looked at the clock, I had been in His presence for 2 hours!"

We, along with many others, have learned that it is not about a physical location. Instead, "Where Heaven Meets Earth" is the place where you know you are in the presence of God and He is impacting your heart, wherever you may be at the moment. We not only wanted to enter there, we wanted to learn how to dwell in the place of His intimacy. We wanted to be aware of His presence all day long and impact our world with the power of His presence so people would know the reality of the Glory of God on earth.

Since everything in life is a continual learning experience, we believe the learning of prayer is a journey. But it's a journey that has been well worth every moment spent with Him. Moments that has at times turned into hours. Moments that have at time happen instantaneously as we focus our attention on Him, no matter where we are. Moments that have caused a shift in our mindset toward spending time with God in prayer. A shift that has taken us from thinking we have a duty to pray, to thinking, "We can't help but spend time with Him."

As we began to study the scriptures on the Tabernacle (in reference to a model for prayer) they came alive in our hearts in a new way, drawing us into the dwelling place of God. It is a journey that continues to deepen our relationship with God as we discover greater depths of our relationship with Him. This journey in prayer causes us to have hope and purpose as we keep our minds intentionally focused on the wonders of God and His plan for our lives and His Kingdom.

Since we are both ministers, we make it our practice to develop our values and habits based on the Scriptures while being led by the Spirit. We discuss, examine, and test what we have learned, as well as how to communicate spiritual revelations in a way that is in line with the person and plans of Jesus.

In this journey each of us must choose not only to begin the process but to persevere to greater understanding. Whether you are struggling with not knowing where to begin in prayer, or wanting to discover greater depths of your relationship with God, we pray the Scriptural truths presented in this Bible study and prayer guide will come alive in your heart.

Welcome to the journey.

Chapter One

Keys to Intimacy and Impact through Prayer

'I urge, then, first of all, that requests, prayers, intercession and thanksgiving be made for everyone.'
(1 Timothy 2:1)

The word of God makes it clear that we are to make prayer a priority in our lives. However, we all have events in our lives that can hinder us from actually spending time in prayer: children crying, emergencies, a sleepless night, sickness, and the list goes on. All of these events are perfectly understandable. And for that very reason it is crucial that we begin our prayer journey by examining things which may hinder our time in prayer.

As you do so, it's important that you do not focus on the times when the above events have hindered you from spending time with God. Instead, focus on those times that you have experienced some level of intimacy in prayer and you have known for certain that your prayers have had an impact on your own life, as well as the world around you.

I. 5 KEYS TO INTIMACY THROUGH PRAYER

Some of the reasons people do not pray are:

1. **They have never set a time and a place to pray**: Set a time before you continue. It may change, but consider it as your starting point.

2. **They have experienced unanswered prayer in the past**: Don't focus on what you feel God hasn't done. Focus on the times you have received answers to your own prayer, or to the prayers of others.

3. **They think it won't really change things**: After reading chapter 2, I believe your feelings toward this reason will change.

4. **They lack a Biblical understanding concerning prayer**: In chapter 3, you will learn about your role in prayer and God's design for you as His representative here on Earth.

5. **They don't know where to begin**: In chapter 4, you will learn principles from scripture that will guide you in your prayer time.

We must all be transparent before God and admit that there are times when we feel God does not hear us. It feels as though there is a disconnect between Heaven and Earth. It is at those times that we must remind ourselves of the following truths found in God's Word. As illustrated below, when the Psalmist felt God was distant from him, he quickly reminded himself of the true character of God.

> **Ps 10:1** says *'Why, O LORD, do you stand far off? Why do you **hide yourself** in times of trouble?'* However, it is then followed by **Ps 10:17** saying, *'**You hear**, O LORD, the desire of the afflicted; you encourage them, and **you listen** to their cry.'*

> **Ps 22:1-2** says *'My God, my God, why have you **forsaken me**? Why are you so far from saving me, so far from the words of my groaning? O my God, I cry out by day, but **you do not answer**, by night, and am not silent.'* However, it is followed by **Ps 22:24** saying, *'For he has not despised or disdained the suffering of the afflicted one; he has not hidden his face from him but **has listened** to his cry for help.'*

In the first 40 Psalms alone there is repeated mention of the times God looks for, hears, and answers those who seek Him.

1. God looks for those who seek Him:

> **Ps 14:2** *'The LORD **looks down from heaven** on the sons of men to see if there are any who understand, any who seek God.'*

Ps 1:6 '*For the LORD **watches over the way of the righteous**, but the way of the wicked will perish.*'

Ps 31:7 '*I will be glad and rejoice in your love, for **you saw** my affliction and **knew** the anguish of my soul.*'

Ps 33:18 '***The eyes of the LORD are on those who fear him**, on those whose hope is in his unfailing love.*'

Ps 34:15 '*The **eyes of the LORD are on the righteous.***'

2. God hears those who seek Him:

Ps 5:3 '*In the morning, O LORD, you **hear my voice**; in the morning I lay my requests before you and wait in expectation.*'

Ps 6:9 '*The LORD **has heard my cry** for mercy; the LORD accepts my prayer.*'

Ps 9:12b '*He **does not ignore the cry** of the afflicted.*'

Ps 18:6 '*In my distress I called to the LORD; I cried to my God for help. From his temple **he heard my voice**; my cry came before him, **into his ear**.*'

Ps 34:15,17 '*The eyes of the LORD are on the righteous and **his ears are attentive to their cry**. The righteous cry out, and **the LORD hears them**; he delivers them from all their troubles.*'

Ps 40:1 *'I waited patiently for the LORD; he turned to me and **heard my cry.**'*

3. God answers those who seek Him:

Ps 3:4 *'To the LORD I cry aloud, and **he answers me** from his holy hill.'*

Ps 9:10 *'Those who know your name will trust in you, for you, LORD, have **never forsaken** those who seek you.'*

Ps 17:6 *'I call on you, O God, for you **will answer me.**'*

Ps 21:1-2 *'O LORD, the king rejoices in your strength. How great is his joy in the victories you give! You **have granted** him the desire of his heart and **have not withheld** the request of his lips.'*

Ps 30:2 *'O LORD my God, I called to you for help and **you healed me.**'*

Ps 34:4-6 *'I sought the LORD, and **he answered me**; he **delivered me** from all my fears.'*

Before you begin your prayer time it is helpful to remind yourself that:

1. **GOD IS LOOKING** (Picture Him looking at you.)
2. **GOD IS LISTENING** (Picture Him attentive to you.)
3. **GOD IS ANSWERING** (Picture Him answering you even though it may not be immediate.)

While contemplating all three of the above truths, remind yourself that you are in the place 'Where Heaven Meets Earth.'

Not only do we need to remove hindrances to the time we spend in prayer, but if we are going to pray effective prayers, we must learn how to remove hindrances to receiving answers to our prayers as well.

II. 10 KEYS TO IMPACT THROUGH PRAYER

The place *Where Heaven Meets Earth* is also the place where we are most certain He is moving by His Spirit, even though we may not see an immediate change in the physical circumstances. It begins in the place where God first moves upon our heart with the revelation of His will, and then moves upon us to work in cooperation with His will and release it in prayer.

Romans 8:26-27 puts it this way. '*The Spirit helps us in our weakness. We do not know what we ought to pray for, but the Spirit himself intercedes for us with groans that words cannot express. And he who searches our hearts knows the mind of the Spirit, because the Spirit intercedes for the saints in accordance with God's will.*'

From the above scripture we learn two important truths concerning prayer:

1. We don't know (in the natural) what we ought to pray for.
2. We must allow the Holy Spirit to teach us.

Do not think that you or your prayers have to be perfect. The truth is that God is not looking for children who never make a mistake. On the contrary, He is looking for children who are eager to learn and have a longing to please Him. When we error, He lovingly corrects us and leads us into the place of meeting with Him so He can teach us His ways.

In the place of intimacy with God, He imparts understanding and grace to follow the leading of His Spirit, both in our prayer time, as well as in our lives. It is in the meeting place with Him that hindrances to answered prayer are removed as we remain open to the leading of His Spirit in the following ways:

1. Be open to the Holy Spirit showing you hindrances in your heart. (Jeremiah 17:9-10, Ps 139:23)

Remember, God accepts you in the place where you are, but He loves you too much to leave you there. He doesn't reveal hindrances in your heart to condemn you. Quite the opposite is true. He reveals what is in your heart to make you more like Him.

> **Ps 24:3-4** *'Who may ascend the hill of the LORD? Who may stand in his holy place? He who has **clean hands and a pure heart**.'*

Ps 66:17-20 *'If I had **cherished sin** in my heart, the **Lord would not have listened**; but God has surely listened and heard my voice in prayer. If I **regard iniquity** in my heart, The **Lord will not hear**. But certainly God has heard me; He has attended to the voice of my prayer. Blessed be God, Who has not turned away my prayer, Nor His mercy from me!'* (I John 1:6-9, 2 Tim 2:22)

Prov 15:8 *'The **prayer of the upright pleases him.**'*

James 5:16 *'Therefore **confess your sins** to each other and pray for each other so that you may be healed. The prayer of a **righteous man** is powerful and effective.'*

What are some of the things in your heart that could hinder your prayers?

A. Un-forgiveness / Wrong Attitudes

Mark 11:25-26 *'And whenever you stand praying, if you have anything against anyone, **forgive** him, that your Father in heaven may also forgive you your trespasses. But if **you do not forgive, neither will your Father** in heaven forgive your trespasses.'* (Eph 4:32, Col 3:13)

1 Peter 3:7 *'Husbands, likewise, dwell with them with understanding, giving honor to the wife, as to the weaker vessel, and as being heirs together of the grace of life, **that your prayers may not be hindered.**'* (I Peter 3:1-6, Timothy 2:1-3, 1 Peter 5:5-7)

Hebrews 4:12 *'For the word of God.....judges the thoughts and attitudes of the heart.'*

B. Hypocrisy

Matthew 6:5-6 *'And when you pray, you **shall not be like the hypocrites**. For they love to pray standing in the synagogues and on the corners of the streets, that they may be seen by men. Assuredly, I say to you, they have their reward. But you, when you pray, go into your room, and when you have shut your door, pray to your Father who is in the secret place; and your Father **who sees in secret will reward you openly.'** (Luke 18:11-14, Philippians 2:3-11, Daniel 10:12)*

C. Selfish motives

James 4:3 *'You ask and do not receive, because you ask amiss, that you may spend it **on your pleasures.'***

D. Pride

James 4:6 *'God **opposes the proud** but gives grace to the humble.'*

When we pray, God compassionately reveals things in our heart that need to be made right. Remember, He is not trying to condemn us. He wants to help us to be conformed into the image of Christ so we can align ourselves with His will. He began this work by forgiving us of sin through His mercy when we received Him as Savior.

He continues this work through His grace as we regularly examine our hearts in prayer. We have only to ask His forgiveness, a prayer He readily hears and accepts.

2. Anticipate that the Holy Spirit will make known to you the will of God.

1 John 5:13-15 *'This is the confidence we have in approaching God: that if we ask anything **according to his will**, he hears us. And if we know that he hears us - whatever we ask- we know that we have what we asked of him.'*

Romans 10:17 *'So then faith comes by hearing, and **hearing by the word of God.'***

John 16:13 *'But when he, the **Spirit of truth**, comes, he will **guide you into all truth**. He will not speak on his own; he will speak only what he hears, and he will tell you what is yet to come.'*

Matt 6:33 *'But seek first **his kingdom** and his righteousness, and **all these things will be given to you** as well.'*

John 6:38-39 *'For I have come down from heaven not to do my will but **to do the will of him who sent me.'***

The focus of our prayers should be our Father's Kingdom. It is the very essence of why we should long to meet with Him Whether we believe that we already know the will of God, or we are seeking Him for His will, we must remember that prayer is not our attempt to convince God to do something. On the contrary, included in the purpose of prayer is the aligning of ourselves with His will.

Leonard Ravenhill said,

"Prayer is not an argument with God to persuade
Him to move things our way,
but an exercise by which we are enabled
by the Holy Spirit to move ourselves His way."

3. Believe that the Holy Spirit will help you to pray in faith.

Matt 21:22 *'If you believe, you will receive whatever you ask for in prayer.'*

Heb 12:2 *'Jesus, the **author and perfecter** of our faith.'*

Matt 13:58 *'And he did not do many miracles there because of **their lack of faith.**'*

Rom 10:17 *'**Faith comes from hearing** the message, and the message is heard through the word of Christ.'*

Faith is not something you work up to. Faith is something you receive as His Word is made alive in you. For this reason it is best to read the Word of God before you even begin to pray. In fact, your entire prayer time should be infused with scriptures which God has made alive to you at some point in your life.

Meditate on any Word that stands out to you and allow His Holy Spirit to pray His word through you in faith. Reword it to fit your situation and it will cause you to pray in faith, as well as to continue in prayer until you have reassurance from the Holy Spirit that He is moving on the prayer need.

You may want to post the scriptures somewhere in your house so you can refer to them often.

4. Trust that the Holy Spirit will give you the grace to be persistent.

> **Luke 11:8** *'I tell you, though he will not get up and give him the bread because he is his friend, yet **because of the man's boldness** he will get up and give him as much as he needs.'*

> **Luke 18:1-8** *'Then Jesus told his disciples a parable to show them that they should **always pray and not give up.**'*

> **Rom 12:12** *'Be joyful in hope, patient in affliction, **faithful in prayer.**'*

> **Col 1:9** *'For this reason, since the day we heard about you, we have **not stopped praying for you.**'*

1 Thess 5:17 *'Pray continually.'*

Biblical Examples: 2 Kings 4:8-37, Daniel 10:2-14, Mark 8:22-26, 2 Cor 12:12

Persistence is not a tool for convincing God to do something. Instead, it is part of the process God uses to mature us and prepare us for the answer. George Mueller said,

> "It is not enough to begin to pray, or to pray aright,
> nor is it enough to continue for a time to pray,
> but we must patiently, believingly, continue in
> prayer until we receive an answer."

Never give up, God's timing is perfect, not only for your situation but also for your heart.

5. Allow the Holy Spirit to work in you to be earnest.

> **Romans 8:26-27** *'In the same way, the Spirit helps us in our weakness. We do not know what we ought to pray for, but the Spirit himself intercedes for us with **groans that words cannot express**. And he who searches our hearts knows the mind of the Spirit, because the Spirit intercedes for the saints in accordance with God's will.'*

> **James 5:17** *'Elijah was a man just like us. He **prayed earnestly** that it would not rain, and it did not rain on the land for three and a half years.'*

Jer 9:1 *'Oh, that my **head were a spring of water and my eyes a fountain of tears!** I would **weep day and night** for the slain of my people.'*

Ezra 10:1 *'While Ezra was praying and **confessing, weeping and throwing himself down** before the house of God.'*

Heb 5:7 *'During the days of Jesus' life on earth, he offered up prayers and petitions with **loud cries and tears** to the one who could save him from death, and he was heard because of his reverent submission.'*

Gal 4:19 *'My dear children, for whom I am again in the **pains of childbirth** until Christ is formed in you.'*

2 Cor 11:29 *'Who is led into sin, and I do not **inwardly burn?'***

So often when we pray we can tend to ask half-heartedly for what we want. But there are times when God is teaching us to value what we are asking for.

6. Expect that the Holy Spirit will bring unity to your home and church.

John 17:20 (Jesus praying for us) *'That all of them may be one, Father, just as you are in me and I am in you.'*

Ps 133:1, 3 *'How good and pleasant it is when **brothers live together in unity!**...For there the LORD **bestows his blessing.'***

Rom 15:5-6 *'May the God who gives endurance and encouragement give you a spirit of unity among yourselves as you follow Christ Jesus.'*

God wants us to be in unity with His Spirit so that we can also be in agreement with other believers. It is then that we can pray for others and receive a blessing for the benefit of all concerned.

7. Entrust that the Holy Spirit will give you grace (enabling power) to listen and obey what He says.

> **Zech 7:13** *'"When I called, they did **not listen**; so when they called, I would not listen," says the LORD Almighty.'* (Jer 15:1, Prov 28:9)

> **1 John 3:21-23** *'Dear friends, if our hearts do not condemn us, we have confidence before God and **receive** from him anything we ask, **because we obey his commands and do what pleases him.** And this is his command: to believe in the name of his Son, Jesus Christ, and to love one another as he commanded us.'*

We can't expect to pray and receive answers if we are not willing to live in obedience to Him. Living in rebellion discredits God and His provision. Living in obedience honors Him and what He does for us.

8. Yield to the abiding power of the Holy Spirit in you for bearing fruit.

> **John 15:7,16-17** *'If you abide in Me, and My words abide in you, you will ask what you desire, and it shall be done for you...go and bear fruit-fruit that will last. Then the Father will give you whatever you ask in my name.'*

We cannot produce spiritual fruit without abiding in the Holy Spirit who produces the fruit of the Kingdom in us. Abiding includes speaking in faith after praying so we are not robbed of a harvest after we pray (Gal 5:22-26, Proverbs 18:21).

9. Allow the Holy Spirit to inspire you to worship in spirit and in truth.

> **John 4:22-24** *'Yet a time is coming and has now come when the true worshipers will worship the Father in spirit and truth, for they are the kind of worshipers the Father seeks.'*

Worship becomes a form or a duty when it is given outside of worshiping as instructed by God – through the inspiration of the Holy Spirit. As we intently focus on God, worship ushers us into His Presence. (This will be covered more in depth in chapter 3.)

10. **Seek guidance from the Holy Spirit to pray in Jesus' Name.** (His Name stands for His authority, power, character, attributes, and renown; and we have been given His Name.)

> **John 14: 12-14** *'Most assuredly, I say to you, "he who believes in Me, the works that I do he will do also; and greater works than these he will do, because I go to My Father. And whatever you ask **in My name, that I will do**, that the Father may be glorified in the Son. If you ask anything **in My name, I will do it."'***

> **John 16:26-28** *'In that day you will ask **in My name**, and I do not say to you that I shall pray the Father for you; for the Father Himself loves you, because you have loved Me, and have believed that I came forth from God. I came forth from the Father and have come into the world. Again, I leave the world and go to the Father.'*

Praying in Jesus' Name means that after meeting with Him, we are changed more into His likeness, and we are enabled to go out into our world as His representatives to impact our world in the same manner Jesus would impact it if His feet were standing on the earth in the midst of your circumstances. What a wonderful privilege! (We will be talking more about this in chapters 3 and 4).

For now, focus on the truth that He wants to meet with you. And while meeting with you He will graciously reveal anything that could hinder your prayers—prayers that have been ordained by God to impact your world.

In addition, do not let the previous list overwhelm you as though you have to examine each one every day to receive answers to prayer. Simply be aware of them and allow the Holy Spirit to reveal anything you need to make right with God. As we will see in the next chapter, it is from this meeting place with God that power will flow to impact your world.

Chapter One Study Guide

Key Verses:

I urge, then, first of all, that requests, prayers, intercession and thanksgiving be made for everyone. (1 Timothy 2:1)

The Spirit helps us in our weakness. We do not know what we ought to pray for, but the Spirit himself intercedes for us with groans that words cannot express. And he who searches our hearts knows the mind of the Spirit, because the Spirit intercedes for the saints in accordance with God's will. (Romans 8:26-27)

1. Of the 5 hindrances to spending time in prayer mentioned at the beginning of this chapter, what would you say has been your greatest hindrance(s)?

2. Of the 10 hindrances to receiving answers to prayer what do you believe is your greatest struggle? What will you do to address this struggle?

3. What three truths do we need to remind ourselves of when we pray (see page 11)?

     1. God is _____
     2. God is _____
     3. God is _____

In your opinion, how can reminding yourself of these three truths inspire you to pray?

Write your personal plan for greater intimacy in prayer:

Chapter Two

The Power of
Passionate, Prevailing Prayer

'Elijah was a man just like us.
He prayed earnestly that it would not rain,
and it did not rain on the land for three and a half years.
Again he prayed, and the heavens gave rain,
and the earth produced its crops.'
(James 5:17-18)

What a comfort it is to know we do not have to be a spiritual giant to pray effective prayers. When you study the story of Elijah, you learn he was an ordinary man who ascertained the will of God and prayed according to what God said. On the following pages you will learn different ways we can ascertain God's will and begin the journey of releasing it on the Earth through prayer. What an exciting journey!

I. TWO SIDES OF PRAYER

1. The Divine (God's part – His will that He wants to release upon the earth.)

2. The Human (Our part – Discerning the heart of God and releasing His will in prayer and in deed.)

There are some events within the Kingdom of God that are His will and are going to happen no matter what we do. For instance, the Son of God is going to return to this earth someday. I can agree or disagree, but it is going to happen no matter what I say. However, there are other events through which God has chosen, in His sovereignty, to work through the prayers and declarations of man, not separate from them. Dutch Sheets put it this way:

"God chose to work through humans not independent of them."

It is clear from scripture that, when we align ourselves with God, He longs to grant us what we ask:

Matthew 18:19 *'Again, I tell you that if two of you on earth agree about anything you **ask** for, **it will be done for you** by my Father in heaven.'*

Matthew 21:22 *'If you believe, **you will receive** whatever you **ask for in prayer.'***

Mark 11:24 *'Therefore I tell you, whatever you **ask for in prayer**, believe that you **have received** it, and **it will be yours.'***

John 14:13-14 *'And **I will do** whatever **you ask** in my name, so that the Son may bring glory to the Father. You may **ask me** for anything in my name, and **I will do it.'***

John 16:23-24 *'My Father **will give** you whatever **you ask** in my name. Until now you have not asked for anything in my name. **Ask** and you **will receive**, and your joy will be complete.'*

I John 5:14-16 *'This is the confidence we have in approaching God: that **if we ask** anything according to his will, he hears us. And if we know that he hears us--whatever **we ask**--we know that **we have** what we **asked of him.'***

II. BIBLICAL EXAMPLES OF GOD GIVING TO THOSE WHO ASK

We have been given the wonderful privilege of being receptors of the will of God, and then releasing His will on this earth. When we believe this reality, it inspires us to pray and not give up until we know we have accomplished what He has called us to do concerning any given situation.

As you read through the following examples of answered prayer in scripture, notice how each of the prayers are according to the will of God in Heaven. However, also notice that, even though each one was according to His will, God moved only after someone had prayed His will on earth.

In these scriptures you will discover the truth spoken by Jack Hayford when he said,

"Prayer is essentially a partnership of the redeemed child of God working hand and hand with God toward the realization of God's redemptive purposes upon the earth."

1. **It was the will of God to fill the Temple with His glory, but Scripture makes note that it happened after prayer.**

    2 Chron 7:1 *'When Solomon **finished praying**, fire came down from heaven and consumed the burnt offering and the sacrifices, and the glory of the LORD filled the temple.'*

    2 Chron 7:11-12 *'the LORD appeared to him at night and said: **I have heard your prayer** and have chosen this place for myself as a temple for sacrifices.'*

Our Heavenly Father wants us know to that we have an amazing destiny which involves us both inviting and releasing His will on the earth. It is not another task to be dreaded but a relationship and privilege to be desired.

2. **It was the will of God to send rain on the earth, but it happened after prayer.**

    1 Kings 18:42-45 *'Elijah climbed to the top of Carmel, **bent down to the ground and put his face between his knees**... Meanwhile, the sky grew black with clouds, the wind rose, **a heavy rain came** on and Ahab rode off to Jezreel.'*

James 5:17-18 *'Elijah was a man just like us. He **prayed earnestly** that it would not rain, and it did not rain on the land for three and a half years. Again **he prayed**, and the heavens **gave rain**, and the earth produced its crops.'*

Elijah had a prophetic word given to him by God, yet he still prayed to see it fulfilled. Too often we receive a prophetic word and then just sit back and wait for it to happen. But the truth is God wants you to experience His power moving through you to release it!

3. It is the will of God to defeat the enemy, but it happened after prayer.

> **2 Kings 19:15-16** *'And **Hezekiah prayed** to the LORD:...**Give ear**, O LORD, and **hear; open your eyes**, O LORD, and **see.**'*

> **2 Kings 19:20** *'I **have heard your prayer** concerning Sennacherib king of Assyria.'*

> **2 Kings 19:35-36** *'...**the angel of the LORD went out....So Sennacherib** king of Assyria broke camp and **withdrew.'***

How exciting to know that we can be used of God to even change the outcome of wars. God sees what is happening and looks for someone who will participate in the release of His victory.

4. It is the will of God to deliver His people, but it happened after prayer.

> **Dan 9:2-3** *'I, Daniel, **understood from the Scriptures**, according to the word of the Lord given to Jeremiah the prophet, that the desolation of Jerusalem would last seventy years. So I turned to the Lord God and **pleaded with him in prayer and petition, in fasting, and in sackcloth and ashes.**'*

> **Daniel 9:23** *'While I was still in prayer,* Gabriel...came to me...**As soon as you began to pray,** an answer was given.'

Daniel received a truth as well as a time frame right from the Scriptures, yet he understood that he still needed to pray. He was willing to be the vessel Where Heaven Meets Earth to bring about deliverance for a nation.

5. It was the will of God to fill Jesus with His Holy Spirit, but it happened after prayer.

> **Luke 3:21-22** *'And **as he was praying**, heaven was opened and **the Holy Spirit descended** on him in bodily form like a dove.'*

> **Luke 9:29** *'**As he was praying**, the appearance of **his face changed**, and his clothes became as bright as a flash of lightning.'*

Even though Jesus was the Son of God, he lived in complete submission to His Father and expressed His submission by asking for whatever was already promised to Him by His Father – even His need of the Holy Spirit. It was the practice of Jesus to glorify His Father through acknowledging Him in prayer. (John 17:1-4, Luke 9:16)

6. It was the will of God to fill the Disciples with the Holy Spirit, but it happened after prayer.

John 14:16 *'And I will **ask** the Father, and **he will give** you another Counselor.'*

Matthew 3:11 *'Jesus **will baptize** you with the Holy Spirit and with Fire.'*

Acts 1:4 *'Do not leave Jerusalem, but wait for the gift my Father **promised.'***

Acts 1:8 *'And **you shall receive** power when the Holy Spirit comes on you.'*

Acts 1:14 *'They all joined together **constantly in prayer.'***

Acts 2:4 *'**All of them were filled with the Holy Spirit** and began to speak in other tongues as the Spirit enabled them.'* (Acts 2:32-33)

The disciples had a promise from Jesus, yet they still had to pray. We can't afford to think that when God gives us a specific promise concerning our need, that we can simply wait on its fulfillment. Instead He wants us to experience the power of declaring His promise with the expectancy that it is going to happen as He says.

7. It was the will of God to send His Spirit to the Gentiles, but it happened after prayer.

> **Acts 10:1a, 2b, 4b,9-10, 44** '*At Caesarea there was a man named Cornelius...; he gave generously to those in need and* **prayed to God regularly**...*The angel answered,* '**Your prayers** *and gifts to the poor* **have come up as a memorial offering before God.**' *Peter went upon the roof* **to pray**...*he fell into a trance...While Peter was still speaking these words,* **the Holy Spirit came on all** *who heard the message.*'

Following the example of Jesus and the disciples, the early church continued to meet with God to seek His indwelling power. They knew by example that it was a relationship to be greatly desired.

8. **It is the will of God to perform miracles, save souls, and deliver, but it happened after prayer.**

> **Acts 2:42-47** *'They **devoted themselves** to the apostles' teaching and to the fellowship, to the breaking of bread and **to prayer**. Everyone was filled with awe, and **many wonders and miraculous signs** were done by the apostles. All the believers were together and had everything in common. Selling their possessions and goods, they gave to anyone as he had need. **Every day** they continued to meet together...**the Lord added to their number daily those who were being saved.'**

> **Acts 4:31** *'**After they prayed**, the place where they were meeting was shaken. And they were all **filled with the Holy Spirit** and spoke the word of God boldly.'*

When we submit ourselves to God, and seek to glorify Him as our Father, He promises to do what we cannot do on our own – wonders and miraculous signs. It is not something we seek as a test for God to prove Himself, but to reveal His love and care for the people He created.

9. **It was the will of God to deliver Peter from prison, but it happened after prayer.**

> **Acts 12:5 – 7a** *'So Peter was kept in prison, but the church **was earnestly praying** to God for him.... **Suddenly** an angel of the Lord appeared and a light shone in the cell. He struck Peter on the side and woke him up. Quick, get up' he said, and the chains fell off Peter's wrists.'*

I have heard the above story mentioned in messages with a focus on the ministry of the angels. But just as important as the fact that Angels released Peter, is the fact that our prayers dispatch Angels. We don't command them, God does, but He does so in response to the prayers of His people.

10. It was the will of God to deliver Paul, but it happened after prayer.

> **2 Cor 1:10-11** *'He has delivered us from such a deadly peril and will deliver us. On him we have set our hope that he will continue to deliver us, as you help us by your prayers. Then many will give thanks on our behalf for the gracious favor granted us in answer to the prayers of many.'*

> **Phil 1:19-20** *'for I know that through your prayers and the help given by the Spirit of Jesus Christ, what has happened to me will turn out for my deliverance.'*

Once we have learned that God in His sovereignty has chosen to work through the prayers of man, it is then that we are most inspired to be the place Where Heaven Meets Earth to impact the world. Andrew Murray put it this way,

> *"Is it not wonderful beyond all thought,*
> *this divine partnership in which God commits*
> *the fulfillment of His desires to our keeping.*

Chapter Two Study Guide

Key Verse:

Elijah was a man just like us. He prayed earnestly that it would not rain, and it did not rain on the land for three and a half years. Again he prayed, and the heavens gave rain, and the earth produced its crops. (James 5:17-18)

1. What are the two sides of prayer mentioned in this chapter?

    1.

    2.

2. Of the 10 examples of releasing God's will on earth given in this chapter name 2 that stood out to you and explain why?

    1.

    2.

3. Write about a time when you believe God inspired you to release His will on earth and you received an answer.

4. In what way has this chapter inspired you to continue in, or deepen, your prayer time?

Chapter Three

God's Kingdom Intercessors (Priests of God)

'You are a chosen people, a royal priesthood,
a holy nation, a people belonging to God,
that you may declare the praises of him who
called you out of darkness into his wonderful light.'
(1 Peter 2:9)

If you are a person who has had the experience of being born again, you are a child of God, and you have been chosen by Him to be His royal priesthood, to enter the presence of the King, your Father. It is there that you grow in relationship with Him, hear His voice, and learn to release the power of His Kingdom here on this earth as His representative.

As you go about your daily routine, living the life He has given you to live, even though you are surrounded by the fallen Kingdoms of this world, instead of being influenced by them, you learn to overcome them through the power available to you as His royal priesthood. When you view yourself in this manner, the power of prayer becomes a part of your daily mindset and purpose here on earth.

That does not mean that we take pride in our position, nor do we become overwhelmed by setbacks. Instead, we humbly come before God acknowledging that our role as His priesthood is part of His plan — to release His will through His children serving Him as His royal priesthood as you will learn in this chapter.

This chapter focuses on the wonderful authority which God has invested in His people to fulfill His will through serving Him as priests of God in His Kingdom. As we will see in the following Scriptures, His priests were to come before Him in His dwelling place to:

1. Pray the will of God, and
2. Proclaim the will of God.

It is for this very purpose that man was created and has been given the authority that we discussed in chapter 2. Read through the following brief, progressive revelation in scripture which reveals this amazing truth:

Gen 1:26 *'Then God said, "Let us make man in our image, in our likeness, and let them **rule over** the fish of the sea and the birds of the air, over the livestock, over all the earth, and over all the creatures that move along the ground."'*

Ps 8:6 *'You made him (man) **ruler over the works of your hands; you put everything under his feet.'***

1 Peter 2:9 *'You are a chosen people, a **royal priesthood**, a holy nation, a people belonging to God, **that you may declare** the praises of him who called you out of darkness into his wonderful light.'*

Rev 1:6 (Jesus) *'has made us to be a **kingdom and priests** to serve his God and Father.'*

Rev 5:10 *'You have made them to be a **kingdom and priests** to serve our God, and they **will reign on the earth**.'*

Rev 20:6 *'They will be **priests of God and of Christ and will reign** with him for a thousand years.'* (This is talking about the Millennial reign.)

Concerning the power that we have here on earth through prayer, Billy Graham said,

"From one end of the Bible to the other,
we find the record of people whose prayers have been answered...
people who turned the tide of history by prayer,
men who prayed fervently and whom God answered."

What an absolutely wonderful privilege, yet awesome responsibility we have been given as the children of God. A position in His Kingdom that is filled with great purpose.

I. THE PURPOSE FOR GOD'S PRIESTS IN HIS KINGDOM

In learning about prayer through the role of the priesthood we must see ourselves the way God intends for us to see ourselves in the economy of His Kingdom. It is not an office on earth in which we serve, but a service submitted to the King in prayer and proclamation.

Through this study, we apply the scriptures concerning the priesthood to our praying because of the progressive revelation displayed throughout the whole of scripture. We will see that the spiritual authority of the priesthood in the Old Testament expands from a selected few to include every one of His followers, or believers; a spiritual authority which was provided by Jesus through His death and resurrection as our Great High Priest which is now available to all believers who are all called to:

- Be His royal priesthood

- Pray

- And proclaim His will

As you read through the following scriptures, notice the progressive revelation of God's plan to include you in His royal priesthood.

1. The house of Jacob was chosen to serve God as His priests in Israel.

> **Ex 19:3-6** *'This is what you are to say to the **house of Jacob** and what you are to tell the **people of Israel:** "you will be for me a **kingdom of priests** and a holy nation." These are the words you are to speak to the **Israelites.'***

Aaron and his sons were chosen to serve God as His priests (Ex 28-29). In reference to the covenant promises, the Priests were to be consecrated for two purposes:

A. They were to Pray (Intercede).

> **Ex 28:9,12** *'Take two onyx stones and engrave on them the names of the sons of Israel...Aaron is to **bear the names on his shoulders** as a memorial before the LORD.'*

> **1 Sam 7:5** *'Then Samuel said, "Assemble all Israel at Mizpah and I will **intercede** with the LORD for you."'*

> **2 Chron 29:11** *'My sons, do not be negligent now, for the LORD has chosen you to **stand before him** and serve him, to **minister before him and to burn incense.'***

Heb 5:1 *'Every high priest is selected from among men and is appointed to **represent them in matters related to God.***'

The purpose of His priesthood was (and we will see, still is) to pray – to carry the needs of people to God; going before Him on their behalf, standing before Him in the Most Holy Place, ministering to Him in worship, petition, and intercession.

B. They were to Proclaim.

Deut 11:29-30 *'When the LORD your God has brought you into the land you are entering to possess, you are to **proclaim** on Mount Gerizim the blessings, and on Mount Ebal the curses.'*

1 Chron 16:23-24 *'Sing to the LORD, all the earth; **proclaim his salvation day after day**. Declare his glory among the nations, his marvelous deeds among all peoples.'*

Neh 8:14-15 *'They found written in the Law, which the LORD had commanded through Moses,...and that they should **proclaim this word** and spread it throughout their towns and in Jerusalem.'*

Ps 68:34 *'**Proclaim the power of God**, whose majesty is over Israel, whose power is in the skies.'*

Ps 96:2 *'Sing to the LORD, praise his name; **proclaim his salvation** day after day.'*

Mal 2:7-8 *'For the* **lips of a priest** *ought to preserve knowledge, and* **from his mouth men should seek instruction**-*because* **he is the messenger** *of the LORD Almighty.'*

Here, we conclude that the proclamation of God's Word has power specifically because it is His Word and carries with it the spiritual authority of His Kingdom. The very proclaiming of God's Word can change the atmosphere and surrounding circumstances.

God's way is for His Word to be proclaimed, be made known and spoken, because it is His way; the same way in which He spoke the world into existence which reveals Him as Creator and authority over everything He has made.

However, as you will see in the following scriptures, the priests failed in their responsibility:

Ezekiel 22:30 *'I* **looked** *for a man among them who would build up the wall and* **stand before me in the gap** *on behalf of the land so I would not have to destroy it,* **but I found none.'**

Hos 4:6-7 *'Because* **you have rejected knowledge, I also reject you as my priests**...*The more the priests increased, the more they sinned against me.'*

Mal 2:9 *'"You have* **violated the covenant with Levi,"** *says the LORD Almighty.'*

Mal 1:10 *'"I am not pleased with you," says the LORD Almighty, "and I will accept no offering from your hands."'*

Heb 8:7-9 *'For if there had been nothing wrong with that first covenant, no place would have been sought for another. But* **God found fault with the people.** *It will not be like the covenant I made with their forefathers when I took them by the hand to lead them out of Egypt, because* **they did not remain faithful** *to my covenant.'*

Little commentary is needed other than to say, people are weak and need the infusion of the Holy Spirit through interaction with God in prayer in order to stay in a place with God where they can be functional. It is little wonder that Jesus said in John 15:4, *'Without me you can do nothing.'*

But this was no surprise to God. In His foreknowledge, even before the foundations of the earth were laid, He had a plan in place: Matt 25:34 says a Kingdom was prepared for us "since the creation of the world". A plan which involved His Son, the One Who would not fail.

2. Due to the failure of man, Jesus came as our Great High Priest and King.

Heb 4:14 *'Therefore, since we have a* **great high priest** *who has gone through the heavens, Jesus the Son of God.'*

Heb 7:22 *'...Jesus has become the guarantee of* **a better covenant.'*** (vs. 16-28)

Heb 9:15 *'For this reason Christ is the mediator of **a new covenant**, that those who are called **may receive the promised eternal inheritance.**'*

Heb 5:6; 7:1 *'You are **a priest forever**, in the order of Melchizedek...This Melchizedek was **king** of Salem and **priest** of God Most High.'* (Note: Ge 14:18-20)

A. Jesus Prayed.

Luke 5:16 *'Jesus often withdrew to lonely places **and prayed.**'*

Heb 3:12 *'Christ is **faithful as a son over God's house.**'*

Heb 5:5-10 *'During the days of Jesus' life on earth, he **offered up prayers and petitions with loud cries and tears.**'*

B. Jesus Proclaimed

Luke 4:1,4, 12 *'Jesus, full of the Holy Spirit, returned from the Jordan and was led by the Spirit in the desert.'* (When facing the enemy of His Father's Kingdom this scripture says that **Jesus answered** by proclaiming the Word of His Father.

Luke 4:14, 18-19 *'Jesus returned to Galilee in the power of the Spirit, He has **sent me to proclaim** freedom for the prisoners and recovery of sight for the blind, to release the oppressed, **to proclaim** the year of the Lord's favor.'*

Matt 4:17 *'From that time on Jesus began **to preach**.'*

C. What were the results?

John 2:23 *'many people saw the miraculous signs he was doing and **believed in his name**.'*

John 4:39 *'Many of the Samaritans from that town **believed in him**.'*

John 4:53 *'Then the father realized that this was the exact time at which Jesus had said to him, "Your son will live." So he and **all his household believed**.'*

John 10:41-42 *'And in that place many **believed in Jesus**.'*

3. The early church followed the example of Jesus.

A. The early church Prayed.

Acts 1:14, 2:4 *'They all joined together **constantly in prayer**, All of them were filled with the Holy Spirit.'*

Acts 2:42 *'**They devoted themselves** to the apostles' teaching and to the fellowship, to the breaking of bread and **to prayer**.'*

B. They Proclaimed.

Acts 4:20 *'We **cannot help speaking** about what we have seen and heard.'*

Acts 5:41-42 *'Day after day, in the temple courts and from house to house, they **never stopped teaching and proclaiming** the good news that Jesus is the Christ.'*

Acts 8:4-5 *'Those who had been scattered preached the word wherever they went. **Phillip...proclaimed the Christ.**'*

1 John 1:2 *'**We proclaim** to you the eternal life.'*

C. What were the results?

Acts 2:43-47 *'Everyone was filled with awe,...**and the Lord added to their number daily** those who were being saved.'*

Acts 4:4 *'But many who heard the message believed, and **the number of men grew** to about five thousand.'*

Acts 5:14 *'Nevertheless, **more and more men and women believed** in the Lord and were **added to their number.**'*

Acts 5:28 *'Yet you have **filled Jerusalem with your teaching.**'*

4. The priesthood of God is now our responsibility and privilege.

I Peter 2:9 *'You are a chosen people, **a royal priesthood**, a holy nation, a people belonging to God, that you **may declare** the praises of him who called you out of darkness into his wonderful light.'*

A. We are all to Pray.

Eph 6:18 *'And **pray in the Spirit** on all occasions with all kinds of prayers and requests. With this in mind, be alert and always **keep on praying for all the saints.**'*

I Timothy 2:1 *'I urge, then, **first of all**, that **requests, prayers, intercession** and thanks-giving be made for everyone.'*

B. We are all to Proclaim.

Acts 1:8 *'But you will receive power when the Holy Spirit comes on you; and **you will be my witnesses.**'*

Rom 15:16 *'A minister of Christ Jesus to the Gentiles with the **priestly duty of proclaiming the gospel of God.**'*

Matt 10:7 *'As you go, preach this message: "**The Kingdom of Heaven** is near."'*

Luke 9:60 *'Jesus said to him, "Let the dead bury their own dead, but **you go and proclaim the kingdom of God.**"'*

1 Peter 2:9 *'that **you may declare** the praises of him who called you out of darkness into his wonderful light.'*

C. What the results should be.

Matt 11:12 *'From the days of John the Baptist until now, **the kingdom of heaven** has been **forcefully advancing**, and forceful men lay hold of it.'*

Acts 3:25-26 *'He said to Abraham, "Through your offspring* **all peoples on earth will be blessed."** *(Note:* **Gal 3:29** *If you belong to Christ, then* **you are Abraham's seed***, and* **heirs** *according to the promise.)'*

Col 1:12 *'to* **share in the inheritance** *of the saints in the* **kingdom of light.***'*

Acts 17:26 *'From one man he made every nation of men, that* **they should inhabit the whole earth.***'*

Matt 28:18-19 *'Then Jesus came to them and said, "All authority in heaven and on earth has been given to me. Therefore go and* **make disciples of all nations."***'*

2 Cor 10:15-16 *'our hope is that, as your faith continues to grow, our* **area of activity among you will greatly expand.***'*

Matt 24:14 *'And this gospel of the kingdom will be* **preached in the whole world** *as a testimony to all nations, and then the end will come.'*

5. **When Jesus returns we will reign with Him in the Millennial Kingdom as priests and kings.**

1 Cor 15:24-25 *'Then the end will come, when* **he hands over the kingdom to God the Father** *after he has destroyed all dominion, authority and power.'*

Rev 2:26-29 *'To him who overcomes and does my will to the end,* **I will give authority over the nations.***'*

Rev 5:8-10 '*You have made them to be a **kingdom and priests** to serve our God, and they **will reign on the earth.**'*

Rev 20:6 '*Blessed and holy are those who have part in the first resurrection. The second death has no power over them, but **they will be priests of God and of Christ and will reign with him for a thousand years.**'*

Rev 21:3 '*And I heard a loud voice from the throne saying, "**Now the dwelling of God is with men**, and he will live with them. They will be his people, and God himself will be with them and be their God."'*

Rev 21:7-8 '*He who overcomes **will inherit all this**, and I will be his God and he will be my son.*'

From the above scriptures we can see God's eternal purpose for His people as priests in His Kingdom, both in prayer and in proclamation. In this role we are to release His power and authority. In order to do so, we must learn to see our experience through the eyes of God, the King of the Heavenly Kingdom. If we see it only through our own eyes we will miss what God wants us to see from His perspective.

As we grow in our understanding concerning the above role we are to fulfill as His royal priesthood, it will transform our minds during and throughout our prayers in this lifetime, and will increase our understanding and the experience of the fullness of His power.

II. THE POWER OF HIS KINGDOM

1. We must realize there are two Kingdoms at work in the world.

   A. God's Kingdom

   Ps 145:13 *'Your kingdom is an everlasting kingdom, and your **dominion endures** through all generations.'*

   Dan 7:27 *'Then the sovereignty, power and greatness of the kingdoms under the whole heaven will be handed over to the saints, the people of the Most High. **His kingdom will be an everlasting kingdom**, and all rulers will worship and obey him.'*

   Luke 8:1 *'Jesus traveled about from one town and village to another, **proclaiming the good news of the kingdom of God.'***

   Luke 17:21 *'The kingdom of God is within you.'*

   B. Satan's Kingdom

   Daniel 10:13 *'the **prince of the Persian** kingdom resisted me twenty-one days.'*

   Eph 6:11-12 *'For our struggle is not against flesh and blood, but **against the rulers, against the authorities, against the powers of this dark world** and against the **spiritual forces of evil in the heavenly realms.'***

1Peter 5:8 *'Our **enemy the devil** prowls around like a roaring lion looking for someone to devour.'*

Rev 2:13 *'I know where you live-**where Satan has his throne.'***

Rev 18:2 *'Fallen! Fallen is Babylon the Great! She has become a **home for demons and a haunt for every evil spirit.'***

These verses help us understand that the world we live in is interlaced with evil, spiritual powers with which we must do battle to bring about the word of God's Kingdom here on this earth.

2. In prayer, we ask for the Kingdom of God to come.

Ps 2:8 *'Ask of me, and I will make **the nations your inheritance.'***

Matt 6:10 *'Your **kingdom come**, your will be done on earth as it is in heaven.'*

2 Chron 7:13-15 *'"When I shut up the heavens so that there is no rain, or command locusts to devour the land or send a plague among my people, if my people, who are called by my name, will **humble themselves and pray** and seek my face and turn from their wicked ways, then will I hear from heaven and will forgive their sin and will **heal their land.'***

Deut 28:12 *'The LORD will* **open the heavens**, *the storehouse of his bounty, to send* **rain on your land in season.***'*

Isa 44:3-4 *'For I will* **pour water** *on the thirsty land, and streams on the dry ground; I will* **pour out my Spirit** *on your offspring, and my blessing on your descendants. They will spring up like* **grass in a meadow.***'*

Isa 45:8 *'You heavens above,* **rain down righteousness***; let the clouds shower it down. Let the earth open wide, let salvation spring up, let righteousness grow with it; I, the LORD, have created it.'*

Isa 64:1 *'Oh, that you would* **rend the heavens and come down.***'*

Acts 2:17 *'In the last days, God says,* **I will pour out my Spirit** *on all people.'*

These verses help us to face the enemy with faith in our God, as the One who is involved with us on this earth to work His plan in our lives individually and collectively as the church, impacting our world with Kingdom power.

3. In proclamation we enforce the Kingdom of Heaven on Earth.

To understand the fullness of the following scriptures it is important to understand that in the Old Testament a city could be conquered at the gate. The gate to a city represented the authority to determine what or who would and would not be allowed into the city. Whoever controlled the gate could control the city.

> **Genesis 24:60** *'may your offspring **possess the gates** of their enemies.'*

> **Isa 28:6** *'turn back the **battle at the gate.'***

> **Isa 45:2** *'I will go before you...I will **break down** gates of bronze.'*

> **Proverbs 21:22** *'A wise man attacks the city of the mighty and pulls down the **stronghold** in which they trust.'*

> **Eph 3:10** *'His (God's) intent was that now, through the church, the manifold wisdom of God should be made known to the **rulers and authorities in the heavenly realms.'***

> **2 Cor 4:4** *'The god of this age has **blinded the minds of unbelievers**, so that they cannot see the light of the gospel of the glory of Christ.'*

> **2 Cor 10:4** *'The weapons we fight with are not the weapons of the world. On the contrary, they have divine power to **demolish strongholds.'***

Acts 26:18 *'to open their eyes and turn them from darkness to light, and from the **power of Satan to God.**'*

Eph 1:18-19 *'**I pray** also that the eyes of your heart may be enlightened in order that you may know the hope to which he has called you, the riches of **his glorious inheritance in the saints.**'*

Our area of activity over which we are to pray in power and authority is our home, neighborhood, church, work, school, and market place. (The model for doing so will be presented in Chapter 4.)

In this process we are instructed by God to be His Royal Priesthood, with His authority, entering His presence to ascertain His will. We are then to live day-by-day, throughout our lives, proclaiming His Kingdom. According to Wesley Duewel, this wonderful authority that we have in prayer is yet to be fully realized by many of His people. He said,

> *"The power of prayer is still largely undiscovered and
> little understood by many of His dear children.
> We live so far below our spiritual capacity,
> our privileges and rights as children of God."*

So how do we enter His presence to seek His will so we can enforce it upon the earth? How do we connect with the Holy Spirit and the Kingdom of God within us, the place Where Heaven Meets Earth? In the next chapter you will find principles you can apply to your time of prayer for that very purpose.

Chapter Three Study Guide

Key Verse:

You are a chosen people, a royal priesthood, a holy nation, a people belonging to God, that you may declare the praises of him who called you out of darkness into his wonderful light. (1 Peter 2:9)

1. According to the scriptures given in this chapter, what 2 things were required of every priest concerning the will of God?

     1. _____ the will of God.

     2. _____ pray the will of God.

2. In your own words, define "Royal Priesthood".

3. Think of ways that you can serve in this role, releasing God's will for your family, friends, neighbors, co-workers, city, and nations.

4. What do you believe is the greatest hindrance people have in viewing themselves in the role of a "Royal Priesthood"?

5. Do you feel that viewing yourself in this role would, or would not, affect your motivation to pray? Explain.

Chapter Four

Entering the Presence

of the

Living God

"One thing I ask of the LORD, this is what I seek:
that I may dwell *in the house of the LORD*
all the days of my life, to gaze upon the beauty
of the LORD and to seek Him in his temple."
Ps 27:4

In this chapter, we will learn God's model of prayer for entering His presence. Remember, it is not about a physical place. Instead, it is a spiritual place that we not only enter as His royal priesthood, but a spiritual position of authority from which we live to bring the impact of His Kingdom to this earth.

Andrew Murray said that prayer is so simple a child can do it, but it's also so complex that we could spend a lifetime discovering its depths. Whether you struggle with not knowing where to begin in your prayer time, or you want to deepen your relationship with the Lord, this chapter is intended to help with both.

In the introduction to this book we told about our own personal journey of learning to encounter the presence of God in a deeper measure during times of personal prayer. What you are about to read is the actual model we mentioned which was taught by Dr. David Yonggi Cho based on the Tabernacle of God.

Fifty chapters in the Old Testament deal with teaching about the physical Tabernacle, a place where only the High Priest could enter the presence of God to make sacrifice for the sins of the people, worship, and intercede on their behalf. In the New Testament **forty-three percent of the book of Hebrews** gives us illustrations of how we can now all draw near to God by the Spirit and grow in our relationship with the Lord.

I. GOD'S HOUSE OF PRAYER

'Have them make a sanctuary for me, and I will dwell among them. Make this tabernacle and all its furnishings exactly like the pattern I will show you.'
Ex 25:8-9

In the following verses we are told that the earthly tabernacle was a shadow of the one in Heaven. That's why God was very specific in His instructions for building it. The earthly, or natural pattern, shows us the way to enter into God's presence today by His Spirit. Read through the following verses in Hebrews which teach this truth:

- **Hebrews 4: 14, 16** tells us that Jesus is our High Priest in Heaven and we are instructed by God to come before Heaven's throne to obtain mercy and grace.

- **Hebrews 6: 19-20** informs us that Jesus is in the inner sanctuary of the Heavenly Tabernacle.

- **Hebrews 8: 5-6** reveals that the earthly sanctuary was only a physical shadow of the one which is still in Heaven where Jesus is today.

- **Hebrews 9:1-5, 8-10** shows us that the earthly tabernacle had furnishings and rooms which revealed the physical way into the Holy Place, until the spiritual way could be revealed.

- **Hebrews 10: 19-23** informs us that all of God's people can now draw near to God in the Holy Place because of Jesus our Great High Priest.

In this section we draw truths from the physical tabernacle which helps us to seek God in the Heavenly spiritual tabernacle. On the following page you will find a diagram which displays four areas in God's House.

Included are the furnishings in each room which symbolize truths that deepen our relationship with the Lord. In the same way that our earthly houses have rooms and furnishings which serve a **natural purpose,** in God's house the rooms and the furnishing serve a **spiritual purpose.** This purpose is expressed in and through us as His royal priesthood, and the dwelling place of His Spirit, to have an impact on our world.

The Rooms/Areas in the Tabernacle	Spiritual Purpose for Drawing Near
1. The Gate	Thanksgiving and Praise
2. The Outer Court	Cleansing
3. The Holy Place	Worship
4. The Most Holy Place	Prayer and Intercession

Below is a simplified diagram of the physical tabernacle. As you look at the diagram, imagine yourself entering God's spiritual house. Following the chart is an explanation for the spiritual purpose for each room and how it relates to us meeting with God. For now, begin at the bottom of the diagram and notice the following progression:

ROOMS FOR DRAWING NEAR	SCRIPTURAL TERMS FOR PRAYER
4. THE MOST HOLY PLACE	Petition, Entreat, Supplication, Travail, Moan/Groan, Tongues, Warfare Requests, Wrestling
3. THE HOLY PLACE	Worship, Adoration, Communion
2. THE OUTER COURT	Cleansing, Confession, Contrition, Repentance, Die Daily
1. THE GATE OR THE WAY	Praise, Thanksgiving

1) **The Gate or the Way**: We enter God's house with a thankful heart for all that God has done for us.

2) **The Outer Court:** Because of what Jesus has done for us, we realize He is a gracious God and are motivated to examine our heart in a time of cleansing.

3) **The Holy Place:** We begin to worship until we know our heart and mind are focused on God.

4) **The Most Holy Place:** We are now ready to begin a time of prayer and intercession.

This process can last a few minutes or can take hours. It's not about the time. It's about intimacy with God that results in His impact upon our world through understanding His model of prayer.

II. DEFINITION OF WORDS RELATING TO PRAYER

Eph 6:18

"And pray in the Spirit on all occasions with all kinds of prayers and requests. With this in mind, be alert and always keep on praying for all the saints."

ENTERING HIS GATES

Thanksgiving: Giving gratitude
Praise: Shout, extend the hand, clap your hands, sing, dance

IN THE OUTER COURT

Confession: To extend the hand for doing wrong
Contrition: To be truly sorry, or contrite

IN THE INNER COURT

Worship: To bow deeply and give homage or reverence
Communion: Indicates fellowship or intimacy

IN THE MOST HOLY PLACE

Petition: To make a request
Entreat: To pray, seek, urge, ask, beseech
Intercession: To plead for, make an appeal on another's behalf
Meditation: To focus on, ponder, or contemplate
Supplication: To make a strong request, made humbly; a passionate pleading
Travail: Pain as associated with childbirth
Fasting: To cover over the mouth, abstain from food
Warfare / Wrestling: An army in spiritual battle, armed

Following is a diagram of the complete tabernacle. The middle column in the chart includes the name of the furniture that was in each of the above rooms/areas. In the left hand column is written the purpose for each room and each piece of furniture under the Old Covenant. In the right hand column is written what the room and the furniture symbolizes for our spiritual relationship with the Lord today.

THE PHYSICAL TABERNACLE	SEEKING GOD IN HIS HOUSE	THE NEW AND LIVING WAY
Only the High Priest could experience the glory of God in the Most Holy Place, once a year to intercede for Israel.	**4. (THE MOST HOLY PLACE)** **The Ark of The Covenant** A Place of **Intercession** In the Presence of God	All believers can now enter the Most Holy Place. It's here that we can all lay our prayers before Him.
Only a Priest could experience communion at the Bread of Presence, keep the Lampstand lit as a symbol of the presence of God's Sprit, and offer worship at the Altar of Incense.	**3. (THE HOLY PLACE)** **Altar of Incense** **Lamp Bread** A Place of **Worship**	All believers can now experience communion with the Lord, be filled with His Holy Spirit and worship God in Spirit and in Truth.
Only a Priest was allowed to wash his hands and feet on behalf of the Israelites to signify daily cleansing before entering the Holy Place. He was also the only one allowed to prepare and make the daily sacrifice of animals for the sins of the people.	**2. (THE OUTER COURT)** **The Laver** **The Brazen Altar** A Place of **Repentance and Cleansing**	All believers can now experience daily cleansing from the influence of sin because Jesus became our sacrifice by shedding His blood once for all.
The entrance gate, also called the way, was the place where the people brought physical offerings as an expression of thanksgiving and praise.	**1. (THE GATE / WAY)** **A place of thanksgiving and praise**	All believers are now to offer a spiritual sacrifice of praise and thanksgiving because Jesus became the Way for everyone to enter the presence of God.

From this point on we will look at each individual area/room beginning with the gate, also called the way. In each of these individual rooms you will notice scripture and commentary for further, personal study on the tabernacle.

III. DRAWING NEAR TO GOD IN HIS SPIRITUAL HOUSE

1. As we enter into His gates and His courts we give Him praise and express thanksgiving.

THE PHYSICAL TABERNACLE	SEEKING GOD IN HIS HOUSE	THE NEW AND LIVING WAY
<u>The entrance gate</u> was also called *the way:* The place to bring offerings (Ex 25:1-7).	1. (THE GATE/WAY) Ps 100:4 Enter into His gates with thanksgiving, And into His courts with **praise**.	<u>Our Gate or Way is Jesus:</u> (John 14:6).

Living with a lifestyle of praise and thanksgiving causes us to enter His house with the right motives and attitude. It also builds our faith to petition Him. However, there will be times when it is helpful, and even needful, to be deliberate in thinking about what He did for us the previous day and be specific in our praise. Too often, we receive what we have prayed for and then go about our life rarely thanking Him for what He has done.

> **Ps 100:4** *'Enter his* ***gates*** *with* ***thanksgiving*** *and his* ***courts*** *with* ***praise****; give thanks to him and praise his name.'*

Ps 118:19-21 *'The gate of the Lord through which the righteous may enter is **giving thanks**.'*

The spiritual application for the gate is that as we come to our time of seeking the Lord, we thank Jesus for being "The way, the truth, and the life."

John 14:6 *'Jesus answered, "I am **the way** and the truth and the life. No one comes to the Father except through me."'*

In addition, think back over the previous day and thank God for what he did for you.

Ps 68:19 *'**Praise** be to the Lord, to God our Savior, who **daily** bears our burdens.'*

Ps 30:12 *'that my heart may sing to you and not be silent. O LORD my God, I will give you **thanks forever**.'*

Ps 106:1-2 *'Praise the LORD. **Give thanks to the LORD**, for he is good; his love endures forever. Who can proclaim the mighty acts of the LORD or **fully declare his praise?**'*

Hebrews 13:15 *'Through Jesus, therefore, let us continually offer to God a **sacrifice of praise**.'*

Phil 4:5-6 *'Do not be anxious about anything, but in everything, by prayer and petition, **with thanksgiving**, present your requests to God.'*

Our goal should be to live a lifestyle of thanking God all day long for what He does for us. Then, when we come to our time of seeking God, our hearts are full of praise and we are humbly moved to a time of examining our hearts.

2. In the outer court we cleanse our hearts.

THE PHYSICAL TABERNACLE	SEEKING GOD IN HIS HOUSE	THE NEW AND LIVING WAY
The Laver: Priest **washed hands and feet to signify cleansing** before entering the Holy Place (Ex 30:17-21, 38:8; Lev 16:4). **The Brazen Altar**: The place for daily **sacrifice of animals** as well as the atonement sacrifice which was once a year (Ex 27: 1-8; Lev 1:1-7:21).	**2. (THE OUTER COURT)** **The Laver** & **The Brazen Altar** A Place of **Repentance and Cleansing** *Ps 24:3-4 Who may ascend into the hill of the LORD? Or who may stand in His holy place? He who has clean hands and a pure heart.*	<u>Our Laver: The Word of God</u> We need **daily cleansing from the influence of sin** in our world around us (Eph 5:25-26; John 15:3; Heb 10:22). <u>Our Brazen Altar: The Cross</u> Jesus became our sacrifice by shedding His blood once for all (Heb 9:22, 10:22; 2 Cor 5:21).

As you will see there were two pieces of furniture in the outer court of the physical tabernacle. First, there was the brazen altar where animal sacrifices were made in the Old Covenant for the forgiveness of sin. The second piece of furniture was the laver where the priests would wash themselves clean for daily sins committed against God.

In the New Covenant, Jesus is the sacrifice for sins. It is His blood that cleanses us from our sins and it is His Word that washes us clean. It all began 2,000 years ago on the cross. However, as you will see in the following scriptures we must repent of that sin. We often talk about how important it is to confess our sins before God, but we neglect to have a focused time of doing so, outside of going to the altar at church. If the pastor doesn't preach about the specific area where we have sinned, we tend to ignore it and eventually sins can end up interfering with our relationship with the Lord.

Remember He is a compassionate and loving God who helps us where we are weak and provides a way for us to be forgiven when we do sin. In the same way He provides forgiveness at salvation, He will provide forgiveness when we sin in our daily lives as a Christian, but we must examine our hearts, and repent.

> **Ps 24:3-4** *'Who may ascend the hill of the Lord? Who may stand in his holy place? He who has **clean hands** and a **pure heart**.'*

> **Heb 10:22** *'Let us draw near to God with a sincere heart in full assurance of faith, **having** our hearts **sprinkled** to cleanse us from a guilty conscience and **having** our bodies **washed** with pure water.'*

Spiritual application for the brazen altar: We thank Jesus for being the sacrifice for our sins. We also think back over the previous day to examine our attitudes, crucify our own flesh, and die daily to ourselves.

Heb 9:14 *'How much more, then, will the **blood of Christ**, who through the eternal Spirit offered himself unblemished to God, cleanse our consciences from acts that lead to death, so that we may serve the living God!'*

Luke 9:23 *'Then he said to them all: "If anyone would come after me, he must deny himself and **take up his cross daily** and follow me."'*

Gal 2:20 *'I have been **crucified with Christ** and I no longer live, but Christ lives in me. The life I live in the body, I live by faith in the Son of God, who loved me and gave himself for me.'*

The second piece of furniture in the outer court was the laver. In the Old Covenant, the priests would wash themselves with the water in the laver to symbolize the washing of the water by the Word of God (Jesus).

Spiritual application for the laver: We cleanse ourselves from daily acts of sin and wash ourselves according to His word.

Ps 51:2 *'**Wash away** all my iniquity and **cleanse** me from my sin.'*

Isa 1:16 *'**Wash** and make yourselves clean.'*

1 John 1:8-9 *'If we confess our sins, he is faithful and just and will forgive us our sins and purify us from all unrighteousness.'*

3. In the Holy Place we worship God the Father through our fellowship with the Son and with the Holy Spirit.

THE PHYSICAL TABERNACLE	SEEKING GOD IN HIS HOUSE	THE NEW AND LIVING WAY
The Altar of Incense was made of acacia wood and overlaid with gold: **Incense** was offered up to God in worship forming a cloud which filled the holy place (Ex 30:1-10, Lev 16:12-13). The Lampstand was made of pure gold and was filled with **oil**: It furnished light for the tabernacle and represented God's presence (Ex 25:31-40; Lev 24:1-4). The Table of Showbread was made of acacia wood covered with gold. On it was placed 12 loaves of **bread**: It symbolized sustenance and communion. (Ex 25:23-30; Lev 24:5-9).	**3. (THE HOLY PLACE)** **Altar of Incense** The Highest Object *John 4:24 "God is Spirit, and those who worship Him must worship in spirit and truth."* **Lamp Bread** A Place of **Worship** Note: When we stand before God at the place of worship, The Holy Spirit and Jesus Help us pray. (Romans 8:26-27, Hebrews 7:25)	Our Altar of Incense is now our **Worship** of God and our Prayers: They are laid before the throne of God where Jesus intercedes for us (Ps 141:2; Heb 7:25, 8:1, 13:15; Rev 5:8). Our Lampstand is **The Holy Spirit** symbolized by the oil: He is the light of Christ which shines in our hearts. (John 8:12; Eph 5:8-11; Matt 5:14-16). Our bread is **Jesus:** He came to us as the Bread of Life. He is the Word of God and The Truth (John 6:27, 29, 35, 48, 51, 63).

In the Holy Place were 3 pieces of furniture:

- **The bread of presence** (symbolizing our fellowship with Jesus)
- **The lampstand** (symbolizing our fellowship with the Holy Spirit)
- **The golden altar of incense** (symbolizing our worship of God the Father)

In The Holy Place, during the Old Covenant, the priest would tend to each of these three pieces of furniture which symbolized communion with God the Son, God the Spirit and God the Father. As the priest would worship God at the altar of incense, he would be ushered into God's presence to begin making his petitions known on behalf of Israel.

At that time, there was a curtain dividing the Holy Place from the Most Holy Place. In the Most Holy Place was the Ark of the Covenant where the glory of God dwelt with His people. Only the High Priest could enter the Most Holy Place and it was just once each year. He would place incense on the golden altar of incense in front of the curtain. The burning of incense would form a cloud, ushering him into the presence of God as he would worship. In the Spirit of Worship, the High Priest would then begin to intercede at the Ark of the Covenant.

In the new covenant, when Jesus died on the cross, the curtain which divided the two rooms was torn. And as His royal priesthood, it is now through a relationship with Jesus, and the indwelling of His Spirit, that each one of us are enabled to worship God in Spirit and in Truth, enter His presence, and then make our petitions known.

In Matthew 6:6-13 and Luke 11:2-4, Jesus gave us the perfect example of preceding our time of petition with worship. When asked by His disciples how they should pray, Jesus said they were to pray in the following manner.

'Our Father in heaven, hallowed be your name **(Ps 141:2** *May my **prayer** be set before you like incense; may the lifting up of my hands be like the evening sacrifice.'* (Rev 5:8, 8:3). There are many ways to worship God. Following is a brief list for the names relating to the Father, the Son, and the Holy Spirit to help you begin your journey.

Choose one name each day. However, for an extended time of prayer (such as an all-night prayer meeting) spend time with an extended focus on each one. As you research each name, and pray through these names one-at-a-time, take notes about personal revelations God gives to you concerning who He has revealed Himself to be.

Worship your Heavenly Father (Altar of Incense)

He is My Righteousness (Tsidkenu)

He is the One Who Sanctifies Me/sets me apart (Mkaddesh)

He is My Peace (Shalom)

He is my God who is always there (Shammah)

He is My Healer (Rophe)

He is My Provider (Jireh)

He is My Banner (Nissi)

He is My Shepherd (Rohi)

Worship Him for His Son (Bread of Presence)

Jesus is the Christ (long awaited Messiah, Deliverer)

Jesus is my Savior

Jesus is my Counselor and Guide

Jesus is my Advocate and Intercedes for me

Jesus is the Author and Finisher of my Faith

Jesus gives me Peace with the Father

Jesus is the One and Only Son of God

Worship Him for His Holy Spirit (Lampstand)

He is the Spirit of Unity

He is the Spirit of Love

He is the Spirit of Light

He is the Spirit of the Lord

He is the Spirit of Wisdom

He is the Spirit of Understanding

He is the Spirit of Counsel

He is the Spirit of Power

He is the Spirit of Knowledge

He is the Spirit of the fear of the Lord

With our focus on the attributes of the Deity through worship, we are then enabled to come before His throne with confidence, knowing He is willing and more than able to meet our need. We are now ready to make our petitions made known in faith and in accordance with His will for His Kingdom.

Up until now we have been deepening our relationship through intimacy with the Lord in Thanksgiving, Confession, and Worship. Now, in the Most Holy Place, Where Heaven Meets Earth in intercession, we begin the releasing of His Kingdom on this earth to have a Divine impact on the kingdoms of this world.

4. In the 4th room (the Most Holy Place) we continue the Lord's prayer with Petition.

Matt 6:10 *'Your kingdom come, your will be done on earth as it is in heaven.'*

Praying here can involve all kinds of prayers such as petition, command, request, and warfare.

In the Most Holy Place we make our petitions known according to the pattern Jesus gave us in John 17 by praying for those closest to us and then working out from there. Be sure to record promises given to you by the Holy Spirit concerning the need you are expressing.

THE PHYSICAL TABERNACLE	SEEKING GOD IN HIS HOUSE	THE NEW AND LIVING WAY
The Ark of The Covenant: Contained the 10 commandments, the rod of Aaron, and the manna. Its lid was made of gold and was called the mercy seat. It was overshadowed by two cherubim at each end. The Shekinah glory of God was between them. It was here that the blood of animals was applied for the atonement of the sins of Israel (Ex 25:10-22, 26:33; 40:34-38; Lev 16:11-22). Only the High Priest could experience the glory of God in the Most Holy Place, once a year (Ex 30:10).	4. (THE MOST HOLY PLACE) The Ark of The Covenant (Luke 11:2-4) A Place of Intercession In the Presence of God *Ps 27:4* *Intercession through the way Jesus Taught us to Pray:* *The Lord's Prayer.* (Entered through a thick veil) *Matt 27:50-51 "When Jesus...gave up His spirit. At that moment the curtain of the temple was torn."*	The Ark of The Covenant is in Our Hearts: The law of God is written on our hearts (Heb 8:10). The rod, symbolizing the Spirit of God, indwells us (Rom 8:11) and Jesus (the Manna) lives in us (John 6:48-51). The blood is applied directly to our hearts (Heb 10:22, Rom 3:25). The Mercy Seat is now the Throne of God which we may approach boldly (Heb 4:16) by the blood of Jesus (Heb 10:19). All believers can enter the Most Holy Place. It's here that we lay our prayers before Him: (Ps 3:4, 5:3, 6:8-9, 10:17, 18:6, Ps 141:2, Rev 5:8, 8:3-4).

The following list is intended to give you a suggested prayer focus for 5 days of the week. Having a list helps us to remember things God has laid on our hearts about which He wants us to pray. However, it is important to be led by the Spirit for the specifics of what He wants us to pray about at any given time.

Monday
Family:

Tuesday
Friends, neighbors, co-workers:

Wednesday
Churches and pastors
Your city and city leaders:

Thursday
Evangelists:
America and it's government:

Friday
Missionaries and nations/leaders:

The return of the Lord and the peace of Jerusalem:

In the remainder of the Lord's Prayer are petitions that prepare us for the day:

Matt 6:11 *'Give us today our daily bread.'* God alone knows what you will need to face the day. But He says we must ask Him for it. (**Matt 4:4** *'Jesus answered, "It is written: Man does not live on bread alone, but on every word that comes from the mouth of God."'*)
(Journal spiritual and tangible needs that you are presenting to the Lord)

Matt 6:12 *'Forgive us our debts, as we also have forgiven our debtors.'* Personal cleansing already took place in the outer court. Here, you ask the Lord to help you live in compassion and mercy for other people you will face during the day, and with whom you may have conflict. (**Luke 6:37** *'Do not judge, and you will not be judged. Do not condemn, and you will not be condemned. Forgive, and you will be forgiven.'*) It is here that we begin to live a lifestyle of forgiveness.
(Journal any wrong attitude in your heart toward others for which you are seeking God's help. To that list, add any person for whom you need the grace of God in your relationship with them.)

Matt 6:13 *'And lead us not into temptation, but deliver us from the evil one.'* Equip yourself for the day ahead. Quote out loud the verses Jesus used to resist temptation in Luke 4:4,8, and 12. (**Eph 6:11** *'Put on the full armor of God so that you can take your stand against the devil's schemes.'* **1 Cor 15:56-57** *'thanks be to God! He gives us the victory through our Lord Jesus Christ.'*
(Journal any area of temptation you are currently facing which involves the three areas Jesus overcame in the desert.)

Matt 6:13 *'For yours is the kingdom and the power and the glory, forever. Amen.'* Remind yourself that as you go forth, you are to be advancing the Kingdom of God, in His power, and for His glory.

(Journal any revelation the Lord gives to you concerning his power to help you with your current circumstances and pray He will receive the glory through answered prayer.)

Conclusion: Just in case you are feeling a little overwhelmed by the extent of this model of prayer from the Old Testament to the New Testament, here is a brief example of what it might look like (specifics omitted).

The Gate or Way of Thanksgiving: *Father, I thank you that your Son Jesus has made the way for me to enter your presence. I am eternally thankful for all that you have given to me* (mention specifics).

The Outer Court of Confession: *In addition to what you did for me yesterday, I thank you for the blood of Jesus that cleanses me and Your Word that keeps me clean. Show me the error of my ways so that I can confess them to you even now* (confess and ask forgiveness).

The Holy Place of Worship: *Because of your forgiveness, I can enter to worship you my Father who is in Heaven. You are my Bread of Presence who is always with me and the Spirit that Lights my Way. I lift my hands in worship to You and glorify your Holy Name* (continue to worship guided by the leading of the Holy Spirit).

The Most Holy Place of Intercession: *You are my God Who makes known to me Your will and empowers me to proclaim your greatness. Guide me as I pray for your kingdom to come and your will to be done here on this earth just as it is in Heaven* (mention your petitions and proclaim His will).

To do your will, I ask you to give me Your daily bread. You alone know everything I have need of today, before I can even ask. And I know that as I share what you give to me with others, there will be enough not only for my physical needs, but also for my spiritual needs.

And as I encounter this world, just as you have forgiven me in the outer court, help me to forgive those I encounter today (ask God to move through you in mercy, grace and wisdom toward anyone with whom you may be having difficulty).

And lead me not into temptation but deliver me from evil. As I go through my day, I will believe you for the grace to not live by bread alone but by every word that proceeds from your mouth, to give my life in worship and serve you alone today, and to refuse to put you to the test by doing things by my own plan.

For yours is the Kingdom, the power and the glory – forever!

From this meeting place with God you are now empowered to go throughout your day in constant communion with Him. As the one who is indwelt by the Holy Spirit, everywhere that you place your feet has the potential for becoming the place *Where Heaven Meets Earth.* You are now God's point of reference for impacting the world.

You are empowered to prophecy, to command, to petition in an instant because you have been in fellowship with the Creator of the Universe. You have aligned yourself with His heart to make known His will in your sphere of influence. You are now His chosen vessel. You are the place *Where Heaven Meets Earth*!

Chapter Four Study Guide

Key Verse:

One thing I ask of the LORD, this is what I seek: **that I may dwell** *in the house of the LORD all the days of my life, to gaze upon the beauty of the LORD and to seek Him in his temple.* (Ps 27:4)

1. List the four rooms/areas in the Tabernacle along with their spiritual purpose for drawing near to God.

The Rooms/Areas in the Tabernacle	Spiritual Purpose for Drawing Near
1.	1.
2.	2.
3.	3.
4.	4.

2. What are the 2 pieces of furniture in the Outer Court which relate to cleansing our hearts before God?

1.

2.

3. What are the three pieces of furniture in the Holy Place which relate to worship?

     1.

     2.

     3.

4. What is the 1 piece of furniture in the Most Holy Place which relates to our petitioning God in His Presence?

5. Think of a way in which the tabernacle model of prayer would help you with the structure of your prayer time, as well as with deepening your relationship with the Lord.

Appendix A:

Scriptures to Guide us In Prayer

Scriptures which say "Pray, Pray for, or Pray that"

Read through the following scriptures and list what is prayed about or for in each scripture. In addition, a Bible Promise book can be a great help in finding scriptures for certain needs. However, remember to seek God for His fresh revelation concerning your specific circumstances. Also, as you're watching the news, talking with people, reading scripture, doing research on the history of your city or church, or merely observing a situation, listen for the Holy Spirit to lead you into prayer (Acts 17:22).

1 Sam 12:23

Nu 21:7

1 Kings 13:6

2 Kings 19:4

2 Chron 6:34-38

Ezra 6:10

Job 42:7-10

Ps 69:13-18

Ps 122:6

Jer 7:16

Jer 29:7-12

Jer 42:2-3

Matt 5:44

Matt 19:13

Matt 24:20

Matt 26:41

Mark 13:18

Luke 21:36

Luke 22:40

Acts 8:22

Rom 1:10

Rom 8:26

Rom 15:31

1 Cor 14:13

2 Cor 13:5-7

Eph 3:14-19

Eph 6:10-20

Phil 1:9-11

Col 1:3-8

Col 4:2-6

James 5:16

2 Thess 1:11-12

2 Thess 3:1-5

Philemon 4-6

3 John 2:2

LEARNING FROM PRAYERS FOUND IN SCRIPTURE

(Read through the following prayers from scripture and note the content of their petition. Note how the prayers are prayed, what they are feeling, the background, and the circumstances.)

Exodus 32:11-13

2 Samuel 7:18-29

1 Kings 8:22-53

2 Kings 19:14-19

2 Chronicles 6:14-42

2 Chronicles 20: 2-4

Ezra 9:5-15

Nehemiah 1:4-11; 9:5-37

Jeremiah 12:1-4

Daniel 9:4-19

John 17:1-26

Acts 4:24-30

Eph 1:15-23; 3:14-19

Phil 1:3-6; 9-10

Col 1:9-12

Philemon 6

3 John 2

Appendix B

Drawing Near in Corporate Prayer

In our travels as evangelists, we have had the blessing of observing several very effective corporate prayer groups. We have noticed that they apply the same core principles of the tabernacle to their prayer meetings (Thanksgiving, Cleansing, Worship, and Petition).

Just as we have an order of service for church, it is also helpful to have an order of service for prayer with an approved individual leading the group in prayer.

1. At home, before coming to prayer:

- ♦ Meditate day and night on the Word – **Ps 119:20, 33-37, 44-48**
- ♦ Come with **Thanksgiving and Praise – Ps 100:1-5**

2. In the prayer session: (The leader should come early and play appropriate music)

- ♦ **Cleansing:** Spend about 15 minutes in private cleansing. (Ps 24:3-4)
- ♦ **Worship:** As you worship, seek the will of God for the night's session. (John 4:24)

- **Intercede:** Make sure everyone knows the leading of the Spirit for the purpose of agreement. (Matthew 18:19-20, I Corinthians 1:9-10, Philippians 4:1-2)

Determining the focus for intercession within a group:

- The leader may have met with the pastor to find the leading of the Lord for that night.
- The leader may receive a revelation directly from the Word of God while in preparation for the evening.
- People within the prayer group may receive a leading of the Spirit. This should be reported to the leader in whatever manner has been predetermined.

Guidelines for selecting a leader:

Understanding of the word of God, committed to Christ, faithful to the house of God, fruit of the Spirit evident, submission to authority, good reputation, agree with church doctrine, filled with the Spirit, and the ability to confront lovingly and lead diligently.

Remain focused on the leading of the Holy Spirit. This may or may not be the time for individual requests. Quite often, personal needs are prayed for at the end of the session.

Cautions for Prayer Groups:

- Don't usurp the authority God has placed over you – **Exodus 17:18-15, I Timothy 5:1**
- Don't become 'super spiritual' – **Philippians 2:3-8**
- Don't expect to always be well received – **Isaiah 30:10-11**
- Don't get discouraged if it's too late – **Jeremiah 15:1**
- Don't gossip – **Proverbs 20:19**

- ◆ Don't stray from clear Biblical guidelines – **Psalms 119:33-37**
- ◆ Don't be swayed by false prophets – **Ezekiel 13**
- ◆ Make every effort to remain in unity – **2 Chronicles 30:12, Psalm 133, John 17:23, Romans 15:5-6, Ephesians 4:1-6, Colossians 3:13-17**

GUIDANCE FOR VISIONS OR PROPHESIES

- ◆ **Revelation – The revelation which comes from God is perfect.**

  2 Sam 22:31 *'As for God, **His way is perfect***; *the word of the LORD is flawless.'*

- ◆ **Interpretation – How we interpret what God wants to say can include error.**

  1 Cor 13:9-11 *'For **we know in part** and **we prophesy in part**, but when perfection comes, the imperfect disappears.'*

- ◆ **Application – We must also be careful how we apply what God has given us.**

  Prov 3:21-23 *'My son, preserve **sound judgment and discernment**, do not let them out of your sight; they will be life for you, an ornament to grace your neck. Then you will go on your way in safety, and your foot will not stumble.'*

- ◆ Test what is said in reference to a revelation from God.

  1 Thess 5:19-22 *'Do not put out the Spirit's fire; do not treat prophecies with contempt. **Test everything**. Hold on to the good. Avoid every kind of evil.'*

- • Don't be insulted if the prayer leader feels what you have said is not what should be prayed about that night.

  Prov 17:10 *'A rebuke impresses a man of **discernment** more than a hundred lashes a fool.'*

- • Prayer is one of the ways in which we test prophesies.

  Jeremiah 27:18 *'**If they are prophets** and have the word of the LORD, **let them plead with the LORD** Almighty.'*

Appendix C

Additional Helps
Concerning Prayer

PROMISES GIVEN TO THOSE WHO SEEK GOD

- Those who seek the Lord **will find Him:**
  Deut 4:29 *'You will find Him if you seek Him with all your heart and with all your soul.'*

- Those who seek the Lord **will rejoice:**
  1 Chron 16:8-12 *'The hearts of those rejoice who seek the LORD!'*

- Those who seek the Lord **will not lack any good thing:**
  Ps 34:10 *'Those who seek the LORD shall not lack any good thing.'*

- Those who seek the Lord **will gain understanding:**
  Prov 28:5 *'Those who seek the LORD understand all.'*

- Those who seek the Lord will **experience revival:**
  > **2 Chorn 7: 14-15** *'If my people, who are called by my name, will humble themselves and pray and seek my face and turn from their wicked ways, then will I hear from heaven and will forgive their sin and will **heal their land.'***

- Those who seek the Lord **will not be forsaken:**
  > **Psalm 9:10** *'Those who know your name will trust in you, for you, LORD, **have never forsaken** those who seek you.'*

- Those who seek the Lord **will receive blessings:**
  > **Matthew 6:33** *'But seek first the kingdom of God and His righteousness, and all these things **shall be added to you.'***

TWO QUESTIONS OFTEN ASKED ABOUT THE LEADING OF THE HOLY SPIRIT IN PRAYER

1. How do you know when the Holy Spirit is calling you to prayer?

- ♦ **An "understanding" from scripture:**
  > **Dan 9:2b-3** *'I, Daniel, **understood from the Scriptures**, according to the word of the LORD given to Jeremiah the prophet, that the desolation of Jerusalem would last seventy years. So I turned to the Lord God and pleaded with him in prayer and petition, in fasting, and in sackcloth and ashes.'*

♦ **A prophecy, dream or vision:**

> **Acts 2:17** *'In the last days, God says, I will pour out my Spirit on all people. Your sons and daughters will* **prophesy**, *your young men will see* **visions**, *your old men will dream* **dreams**.*'*

> **Acts 9:10** *'In Damascus there was a disciple named Ananias. The Lord called to him in* **a vision**, *"Ananias!"'*

♦ **A "burning" in your Spirit:**

> **Luke 24:32** *'They asked each other, "Were not our* **hearts burning within us** *while he talked with us on the road and opened the Scriptures to us?"'*

♦ **The voice of the Lord and the Spirit:**

> **Acts 10:15** *'The* **voice spoke** *to him a second time, "Do not call anything impure that God has made clean."'*

> **John 16:13** *'But when he, the* **Spirit of truth**, *comes, he will guide you.'*

> **1 Sam 3:9, 1 Kings 19:12-13**

♦ **A "troubling" in your spirit:**

> **Dan 7:15** *'I, Daniel,* **was troubled in spirit**.*'*

> **Rom 9:2** *'I have* **great sorrow and unceasing anguish** *in my heart.'*

2. How do you know when you are to stop praying?

The same scriptures which apply to God speaking to you to pray, apply to a "knowing" that you are released from praying. Of course the most obvious indication is a knowledge that the circumstances have changed.

Note: When you are first used of God to intercede, it may be on rare occasions.

- **Luke 16:10** '*Whoever can be trusted with very little can also be trusted with much.*'
- **Matt 25:23** '*You have been faithful with a few things; I will put you in charge of many things.*'

FORMS OF WORSHIP AND POSITIONS FOR PRAYER

Dancing - Ps 150

Kneel and Bow - Ps 95:6

Singing - Ps 7:17

Face to the ground - Luke 5:12

Clapping - Ps 47:1

Sitting – 1 Chron 17:1, Luke 10:39, Acts 2:2

Kneeling – Ps 95:6, Eph 3:14

On your Face – Ezra 10:1, Rev 11:16

Prophetic Acts – Neh 5:13, Isa 20:3; Ezek 4, Acts 21:11

Going about the altar – Ps 26:6

RECOMMENDED READING

Andrew Murray: Absolute Surrender. The Holiest of All. With Christ in the School of Prayer

Leonard Ravenhill: Why Revival Tarries, Revival Praying

Paul Billheimer: Behold I Give Unto You Power, Destined for the Throne

Billy Graham Angels: God's Secret Agents

Wesley Duewel: Touch the World Through Prayer, Mighty Prevailing Prayer

Dutch Sheets: Intercessory Prayer

ADDITIONAL RESOURCES FROM TWIFORD MINISTRIES

Loving Your City (Manual and Conference)

Eating with Purpose (Manual and Seminar)

Information concerning these resources can be obtained at twifordministries.com or by writing: twifordministries@gmail.com